MAFIA, STATE, ART
KISS KISS KILL

Eric Engle

Copyright © 2020

amazon.com/author/quizmaster

INTRODUCTION

A good story starts with a killing or a kiss. It then explains its causes and consequences.

Is the state nothing but a mafia?
This book will help you answer that question so you can enjoy – or avoid! – state power.

Aristotle, Confucius, and Mao Zedong had definite ideas about Art, State Power, and Crime. If we look at their ideas about man, the state, and war in the context of the war of criminals and the state then we may gain some useful insights about the exact contours of the problem of contemporary criminality. Hopefully that may provide insights for people to avoid or extinguish criminality and attain what Aristotle called "the good life".

This small book started as a dialogue with a Chinese artist. I was trying to answer certain questions about organized crime in the USA, art, and state power.

Dedication:

To Wit: Purge early, purge often, and above all purge them before they purge you!

TABLE OF CONTENTS

Introduction 2
Table of Contents 3
Chapter 1. Aristotle, Mao, and Art: The Mafia Myth ... 4
Chapter 2. Aristotle & Confucius 12
Chapter 3. Public Law. Private Justice? 14
Chapter 4. Is the State nothing but a Mafia Writ Large? 18
Chapter 5. Conclusion 27
About The Author 30
Other Books By Eric Engle 31

        Copyright Eric Engle. 2020.

Chapter 1. Aristotle, Mao, and Art: The Mafia Myth

Like I wrote, a good story starts with a killing or a kiss. It then explains its causes and consequences. That's brief but clear and explains why myths and stories, mysteries and histories, about the clash of crime against the State will be perennial, whether as warnings or fantasies. However, that is just what such stories nearly always turn out to be: mere myths.

Why are so-called wiseguys, mafia, organized crime, the sources for inspiration of some of the best cinematic art ever? Because kiss, kiss, kill!

But that doesn't make these intriguing tall tales true.

The first thing to understand about story-telling is that **a story does NOT have to be at all factual to be compelling!**

Just like myths about "organized" crime serve as a great foil for eternal human issues of love and hate, fear and desire so also do stories about dwarves, elves, dragons and the like similarly serve as the source of inspiration for great art! These myths also serve as foils for bringing out broader social and economic conflicts, a form of veiled discourse.

Once we understand that most stories and legends about organized crime are myths along the lines of fairy tales they become more tractable, deflated of bravado and false glamour. Then we can analyze them critically and objectively, rather than be taken in by the glitz and glimmer of the (anti?) heroic and glamourus.

Myths can be sources of inspiration for great art precisely because they are not factual. Mafia legends and mythologies make great vehicles for those who wish to escape from reality in art or imagine living out their dreams and fantasies.

Yet, mythic portrayals, whether of mafia clans or dragons' lairs, can be more than mere escapism, the penny dreadful, pulp fictions. Myth can compel as a metaphor with meaning. Suddenly the struggle between the elves and the trolls, or between the police and thieves become a canvas upon which other conflicts can be painted and safely discussed. In other words: *the more repressive the regime, the likelier metaphors of conflicts portrayed as myths are to serve as vehicles for political struggle.*

Artistic representation can indirectly address issues which otherwise cannot be discussed in authoritarian states. Consequently:

All art is potentially subversive.

MAO ZEDONG

Like nazi propanda minister Josef Goebbels, Mao Zedong understood and directly addressed the central role which propaganda must play in a political movement. Mao described his views on the fundamentally political nature of all art in his "Talks at the Yenan Forum"

Art is as Mao said:

A distillation and compression of real life contemporary issues accentuated to emphasize and expose the underlying truths.

Mao also held that: **All art is political.**

Aristotle

Seeing the political nature of all art is nothing unique to would-be dictators. Plato in *The Republic* and then Aristotle addressed the importance of art to state power. Aristotle states, I think correctly, that art is political and that the purpose of art in the state is:

TO EXTOL AND INSTILL VIRTUE & EXPOSE AND PURGE EVIL FROM THE BODY POLITIC.

According to Aristotle the cathartic function of art is to evoke undesired emotions and purge the audience of them. The relief the audience should feel at the resolution of conflict in the story affirms the auditors' sense of justice. Whether for Aristotle or Mao Zedong *art is central to state power.*

The fundamentally moral and political qualities of artistic representation explain why late modern attempts at narrative skepticism, moral neutrality, amorality, in short the varieties of relativism, ultimately lack persuasive power and will fail. Moral relativism, "value neutrality", will ultimately be exposed as an over-reaction to the world wars and as inaccurate and thus inapt to guide human behavior. Moral relativism, an over-reaction, has already encouraged or at least tolerated unhealthy behaviors like the entire self-indulgent drug culture, obesity, the decline of self-discipline and the consequent fall of culture. However, this decline is literally a "first world problem": supposedly less developed cultures, where the struggle to survive is real do not tolerate encourage or desire liberal hedonism. The rise of the developing world will increasingly challenge the self-indulgent amoral developed world and will discipline the first world if only by the logic of war, international conflict, and economic competition.

As well as pointing out the central moral role of art in the state, Aristotle also regarded the state itself as central to human survival and the pursuit of the good life.

Aristotle said:

"The state comes into being to assure the necessities of life, but continues in existence to secure the good life."

Aristotle didn't say this: I do.

Unlike any mafia anywhere ever.

Whoever argues that the state can or should be abolished is a fool or a liar: people are by nature inherently capable of violence. Those who lack self-restraint will inevitably seek to take advantage of others by force. Thus, state power is necessary if only as a remedy for the moral failings of individuals to respect others.

If "organized" crime (who organized them?) is dysfunctional, unproductive, incoherent, and inefficient why do legends and myths about criminal conspiracies compel audiences' attention? Simple: kiss kiss kill! People are by nature social and have inherent desires to survive and prosper. Fight or flight, mate or die. These fundamental drives, and the distilled concentrated character of art, explain why myths and legends abound in art.

A Subjective View: Huang Mei Opera

Let's look at it subjectively: Personally speaking, my favorite stories are myths about a snake spirit who studied daoism, and was then transformed by her hard work into a human, and then fell in love with some poor geeky med student, only to get chased around by some obsessive possibly deluded religious radical who broke up her loving family: an obsessive maniac and the entire culture he represented ruined a perfectly good albeit strange family! This is the legend of lady white snake, a glorious romance on the order of Shakespeare. It is portrayed most famously in of Huang Mei opera, a popular art form by women tea pickers in China.

I love Huang Mei opera because it is:

the voice of the poor!

the voice of women!!

the voice of love!!!

All that IS the fundamental nature of great art:
Great art is the voice the voiceless.
And, at times, organized criminal groups claim to be the voice of the voiceless.
Artists articulate and express ideas which the audience is unable or unwilling to air publicly and do so in a compelling form.

I love Huang Mei opera because It is culture of the oppressed and exploited. Most everyone roots for the underdog, because people by nature want to be each others' peers. The struggle for equality and excellence is fundamental to that which is truly human.

I also love Huang Mei opera because the love expressed in it is *universal* and this too qualifies great art: it has a message which reaches all auditors, a *universal* message. Huang Mei is:

The love of one's ancestors!

The love of one's children!!

The love of one's life!!!

All of these themes run throughout great literature: historical circumstances, familial circumstances, and individual passions are the common threads of all drama. They are tied together by the struggles for equality and excellence and the varieties of human love: filial, agape, romantic, patriotic, religious, This is true whether our mythic heros and villains are dragons and dwarves or police and thieves.

Because art itself is mythic artistic narrative need not be factual to be compelling. In fact, the counter-factual nature of art can be its strength. The legend of Lady White Snake, is amazing BECAUSE it is fantastic – they have MAGIC POWERS! Who would not want to be able to fly, to turn invisible, or any of the other magical things mythical characters can do? As to criminals, who wouldn't want to be able to defy the law, to roll in riches, to take by force what others must work for?
But the latter are dangerous deadly myths.

Huang mei opera is amazing because it is art Mao said art is:

A distillation and compression of real life contemporary issues accentuated to emphasize and expose the underlying truths.

Art is a bit about myth-making. Myths also sometimes (often?) feature in the political.

Chapter 2. Aristotle and Confucius: Human Nature and State Power

My favorite philosophers are Aristotle and Confucius. They write well, and I find their ideas attractive and their arguments compelling. Many Westerners are unaware of Confucius and I suspect many Easterners are unaware of Aristotle. So I think comparing Aristotle and Confucius is both interesting and useful. Comparing Aristotle and Confucius enables us to see how their ideas influence the political and understand how they relate to Mao's idea about the role of art in political society, which helps us to understand why the state is not in fact a mere band of criminals.

Aristotle teaches that **all men** by nature **desire to know**, and **desire the good**. We are a rational talking social animal, inherently curious, and desiring the good life, according to Aristotle, views which I agree with. However, even though we all, by nature, desire that which is good we do not necessarily know what the good is or what is good for us. But we all chase what we believe to be good, what we desire. Schiller says that too: all desire happiness.

Aristotle's claim that all of us desire the good fairly well corresponds to Confucian thought: "Man at birth, is quite good, but by choices, they diverge" (三字经): people start out basically good, desiring the good, but then by their practices they acquire habits. These newly acquired habits may be good or bad. Aristotle likewise emphasizes the idea of habit as the source of excellence. The proverb goes "Sow an action, reap a habit. Sow a habit, reap a character. Sow a character reap a destiny."

Aristotle also wrote: "man, when perfected, is the best of animals, but, when separated from law and justice, he is the worst of all; since armed injustice is the more dangerous, and he is equipped at birth with arms, meant to be used by intelligence and virtue, which he may use for the worst ends. Wherefore, if he have not virtue, he is the most unholy and the most savage of animals." This is very similar to the Confucian idea of human nature: "If they do not study, they cannot know justice." (三字经) Aristotle also says that all people by nature desire to know, they are inherently curious.

People have desires and they have power. If their desire is properly crafted they attain civilization. But if it is not, or worst of all if it is deformed, then they are genocidal slavers, cruel, mean spirited, greedy, full of hate, in various combinations depending on the degree and type of their deformation.

Confucian ideas about human nature are much more accurate and healthier than the Christian "original sin". Man is born GOOD and is PERFECTIBLE -- but only through much hard work.

Much of what Confucius teaches matches up with Aristotle's ideas.

People are not born as a tabula rasa, a blank slate. We are born like all animals with certain instinctive automatic reactions. Humans have survived and prospered as a species because of our inherent desire to be social. Our social instinct is proof that we are basically good. We don't WANT to be genocidal slavers, hateful hermits, mass murderers, serial killers, or anything other than happy: but many people don't know other better ways or believe themselves trapped in a world of nightmares.

No matter your nightmares what your nightmares are: you are not trapped.

A rational talking social animal, curious, desiring to know, and desiring the good. So Aristotle describes humans.

With this brief understanding of human nature as described by Aristotle and Confucius we can now look to the relationships between justice, law, and the state.

Chapter 3. Public Law or Private Vengeance?

There is law and there is justice. They are different, but may be related in some way. The legal minded believe (public) law may work justice more effectively than private vengeance. Private acts of vengeance, whether blood-feud, clan war, weregeld or other forms of private vengeance such as the secret Vehm courts, are all examples of private claimants of right and justice. These were all normal and legal in pre-modern states, in antiquity. Public law experts argue that monopolizing lawful violence in the "hands" of the state reduces violence and works justice more effectively than private vengeance. However, such private vengeance might be formally or informally ordered.

There is of course the opposite view; it is a view held by various mafia, many criminals, but also by clans, tribes, in short proto-states from the pre-scientific era: the idea that public law is flawed and that any justice can only be obtained by private actions, generally via vengeance.

The idea that public law is better than private vengeance to more closely reach justice is definitively an aspect of modernity. So are limited wars, as opposed to total wars, and for similar reasons. The state in modernity seeks to use violence to reduce the use of violence by monopolizing violence.

As to those who believe that private vengeance is better and more fair than public law at approaching the impossible goal which is justice (life is inherently unfair), who am I to disagree? I am not the state. I am well aware of the failures of state power to attain justice. Then again, the statists argue in extremis, that the primary goal of state power is to impose the monopolization of violence, not to work substantive justice. The state in that view merely imposes order, not justice.

So there are sensible reasons for which one might take the side, e.g. of a given mafia, a group of so-called criminals, for it is only the state's laws which make them criminals, no?

That is not my own view: I believe substantive justice is better attained by public law rather than private vengeance. Then again, in the face of the failure of state power, as was the case in Sicily some 200 years ago, one can well understand why private persons might make justice a private affair. The problem is, then they are, knowingly or not, contenders for state power. And the state claims the monopoly of lawful violence.

Substantive justice is an ideal; it can never be attained. Life is inherently unfair. Is it fair that people die? No. But we cling to the hope of justice, the promise of fairness in our dealings with other people precisely because sickness, death, and natural disasters, are so arbitrary and unfair. Yet we believe, perhaps are naive, that by regulating our affairs as to voluntary transactions we can best cope with a bad situation. For there is a fundamental difference between the death at the hands of a robber or rapist as opposed to a natural or even accidental death through the forces of nature, which until recently were ever more powerful even than the state.

I think the better view is that we come closest to reaching the impossible ideal of justice through public laws rather than by private acts of vengeance. This is definitively the position of modernity. No state in modernity permits blood feuds, duels, or even declares people as out-law, and thus subject to no state protection from private violence. States in modernity likewise suppressed piracy, slave-trading, and mercenarism as challengers to the efficient use of violence by the state, only. All of these legal reforms came with modernity and replaced contrary rules and customs from the medieval era.

Chapter 4. Is the State nothing but a Mafia Writ Large?

Is the state nothing but a mafia writ large? This question certainly is not new. However, at least in a just state, the state is not in fact a mafia writ large.

The problem of criminality, from the criminal's perspective, is the problem of loyalty. Criminal organizations face a number of problems: treachery, deception, cruelty, vengeance, and secrecy - or more accurately the lack thereof. People are social animals and require and desire approval and praise. Consequently, people are generally very bad at keeping secrets. Furthermore, because humans are a social animal, who desire praise and approval by others, we tend to seek fame and fortune. Obviously, famous criminals are likelier to get caught. Wealth once acquired is spent, often ostentatiously, which of course attracts attention of the authorities, whether in tax or policing.

Because people tend to be bad at keeping secrets due to their search for approval, praise, and fame, just about everyone reveals their secrets, sometime, to someone. Thus, it is no really difficult thing for the state to get informants among criminals, whether by appealing to the very greed which motivated them to enter organized crime, or simply the all-too-human desire for fame or approval: "you were bad, but now that you are turning state's evidence you are good".

Whether for love or desire, drugs or other addictions, the various psychological weaknesses of people are there to be exploited by an effective criminal investigative service. Convincing people who are already corrupt to turn against their corrupters and compatriots is not so difficult as in myths.

As well as the problem of the lack of secrecy due to the desire for fame and fortune any criminal organization faces the problem of betrayal. Every mafia boss has underbosses who are literally gunning for the job, their potential assassin.

Criminals' only real loyalty is to themselves, to greed. All mythic illusions, imagery, and show to the contrary, in the end: criminals confess and turn state's evidence in search of leniency. Or in their own words: they rat each other out.

As to the state, What differentiates it from a mafia?

Well, at least as to just states - plenty!

What is the mafia's business model? Crime! Crime for profit!

Does that seem like a sustainable thing? Or is it inevitably doomed and ultimately self destructive? Is crime-for-profit a model capable of replication, of reproduction? Not really.

Crime for profit is basically an unsustainable business model, especially since state's can change the rules to make some profitable crimes no longer criminal -- or immunize criminals who smartly choose to turn state's evidence, enter witness protection, etc.

State power, unlike crime-for-profit, is sustainable because it is predicated on creating a rule system which fosters productive labor and suppresses violence. That is entirely unlike organized crime, which is fundamentally unproductive, even counter-productive.

Consider typical revenue streams of organized criminal conspiracies: examples include robbery and burglary, extortion, gambling, prostitution, drug-dealing and illegal arms dealing. Robbery, like the other examples, does not produce but only redistributes wealth. In fact, robberies discourage formation of wealth: why produce if it will only be stolen? Extortion, "the protection racket" is likewise unproductive since the "protectors" do not in fact protect but merely extort, unlike the state. Gambling likewise merely redistributes wealth and does not produce it. Prostitution? Productive? Of what? Of rapes? Drug dealing likewise produces no new wealth but does incapacitate potential wealth producers and ties down state resources in rehabilitation, hospitals, and grave-diggers: it is counter-productive. People all drugged out on opium / heroin / name your drug are generally not very productive. Most organized criminal activities are unproductive or even counter-productive.

Unlike organized criminal groups the state isn't a conspiracy of lying murderers bent on preserving their own power at any costs.

The state is the family writ large, in most countries: the USA is a big exception. In the USA the state is more like a multinational corporation than the family writ large because the citizenry in the USA is genetically quite diverse, unlike most other countries, where the state is essentially a clan, an extended family But the state-as-family isn't a crime family: it's farmers, merchants, industrialists and workers, not extortionists, robbers, rapists, and murderers. Unlike criminals, states try to monopolize violence to reduce violence and foster productivity and so states tend to exercise restraint in their arms dealing.

So, organized crime is fundamentally unsustainable, unlike the state. The state is not a mere mafia writ large.

Romanticized views of organized crime are as laughably bad as James Bond films in their portrayal of covert violence.

Now that we understand the significance of art as inspiration and the purpose of art as the vehicle of virtue we can examine organized crime and its mythic portrayal in American cinema.

Famous Films About Organized Crime

Although art tends to exaggerate and speak metaphorically about problems beyond the individual characters nevertheless some films about organized crime are worth watching for at least a rough outline of the operations of organized crime. The following films are, at least to some extent, roughly accurate and in all cases are fascinating studies in criminality.

The Untouchables: Prohibition and Bootlegging

Once Upon a Time in America: Labor Union Corruption

Goodfellas NYC, 1950-1985

The friends of Eddie Coyle Winter Hill Gang, Boston

Black Mass Winter Hill Gang, Boston

Brother Russian organized crimein the 1990s

Lord of War International arms trafficking 1990s

These films provide an accurate, albeit historic, perspective on organized crime. Once upon a time in America is actually borderline; it does accurately portray the violence of 1920s organized crime and the penetration of labor unions by organized crime but overplays the degree of influence and power organized crime had. Did you ever notice that labor unions in America are basically non-existent and powerless? That's no accident. Also borderline accurate are the telefilms *Gotti* and *Boss of Bosses*.

In contrast, *Raging Bull, Sopranos, Godfather, The Irishman, Brother 2* struck me as sufficiently unrealistic to be more fictional than factual, even as pastiches or metaphors.

Myth and Truth about Organized Crime & the State:

Criminal organizations don't really exist for hundreds of years. What does exist is legends and myths, which are then acted out by desperate and immature people; depending on how corrupted the state is, those people are all eventually exposed and jailed or killed. The truth comes out in the end, and then what? Witnesses testify, often betraying their former partners' in crime. No criminal can shoot, intimidate, or bribe everyone. Organized crime really is fundamentally weak. However, a corrupted state, especially a corrupted police, can use one criminal faction to control other would be criminals. That sometimes happens, but when it does it only does so in a corrupted state.

Where is Paul Manafort? Where is Mike Cohen? These are the more sophisticated examples of organized criminals; less sophisticated ones you've never even heard of and are already dead or in jail. But let's look at more corrupted states? Where is El Chapo?

Although a criminal faction might exceptionally have its members in government, actually wielding state power, corrupted officials generally get exposed and eliminated eventually, whether by other criminals or their political rivals.When you more or less declare yourself as the enemy of the law you should be unsurprised to find few friends few allies and few options.

The Japanese yakuza are a famous and interesting example. They only exist because they either made the U.S. occupation of Japan a bit easier or as a resistance to U.S. occupation. Yet, what exactly does yakuza mean? It means "losing hand" of cards. Yakuza themselves - you can talk to them they respect that - will tell you they lead miserable lives in the shadows of power performing nasty necessary jobs with the tolerance, and no more than that, of the forces in real power.

Likewise, even a superficial reading of the biographies of the more famous, or even not so famous, criminals in the USA reveals that just about all the "organized" criminals die or end up in jail. Really.

The naive view that organized crime is wealthy, powerful, glamorous, is common but naive. The state is generally happy to have believers in the mafia mythology: when people are tempted to go down a path of selfish dishonest violence - why stop them? Especially if it will assuredly lead them to jail or death?

Although organized crime groups certainly exist, they are not particularly powerful nor institutionalized. The legends of centuries of traditions rituals and roles are just that: romanticized legends. In reality, criminal conspiracies are generally loose associations of violent desperate losers willing to lie cheat steal and kill. Criminals generally are very bad at forethought with low impulse control. They are at most tolerated by those in real power, but criminal conspiracies almost never become institutionalized and always live in peril from the government and their "colleagues". Organized criminal groups only have any traction in corrupted/conquered states, which are generally impoverished, backward, desperate, and thus violent. Examples include Sicily, Russia, and perhaps rural tropical regions where narcotics grow. Japan is the interesting case because of their culture and history. Probably the yakuza will evolve into a fraternal social club. This is because states are increasingly legalizing things like pornography, prostitution, gambling, even soft drugs, all of which are traditional sources of revenue for organized crime. Anything even like a sustainable business model gets legalized in part to destroy and coopt organized criminal groups: Lure away the stupid greedy ones, isolate the violent vicious ones destroy the latter reform the former. That's war, and it works.

But let's suppose that the monopolization of violence by the state does not work substantive justice. Even if the monopolization of violence by the state merely imposes a peace of the strong over the weak domestically, the fact is states attain domestic order (not justice) better than clans, tribes, or contending mafias. Private vengeance is a less effective organizing principles for state power, which is why the state is such a successful form of social organization. Which is better for a society, limited state directed violence or unlimited private violence? I do not speak here of individual justice, only of the society, not of any individuals.

The better question is whether one ought to seek to take state power or instead to avoid state power. I think though these are questions of taste and character rather than of morality.

In my own life I have done the latter. I expect contenders for state power must confront and possibly employ lies and violence. I prefer a quiet peaceful life with perhaps some capacity to influence the state and its laws to a noisesome, perhaps dutiful, life in the public eye.

Chapter 5. Conclusion

I have tried to show the parallels between organized crime and the state, which explain why people may rightly ask whether the state is nothing other than the mafia writ large. The state is not merely a mafia writ large.

To recap, the state and organized crime are both violent and, roughly speaking, are extensions of the family. Sometimes, like the state, organized crime claims to work substantive justice, usually against the backdrop of a failed state, at least in modernity.

However, the differences between the state and a band of criminals are important. The "business" model of organized crime is generally not sustainable or productive. Furthermore, organized crime does not and cannot claim to use violence to limit the use of violence. In contrast, the state monopolizes violence and uses its violence to prevent and limit violence. State power, unlike organized crime, seeks to foster productive labor. Thus, the state is sustainable, unlike organized crime. There is a reason we live in a world dominated by large public law bodies, states and federations, as opposed to a lawless borderless world dominated by competing clans in constant blood feuds.

In greater detail: What makes the just state somehow different than a robber or a criminal gang? Given that the state and the rights it creates and upholds are legal fictions, abstract formalizations imposed to describe reality, why are laws other than arbitrary? Why must/should/does the state use logic to determine its laws?

Laws are logical to be persuasive so that the system is perceived as just and thus becomes a self-enforcing, self-policing, and self-reproducing foucauldian panopticon. Good laws persuade judges and the general public that the outcomes they generate are fair. The state and its laws *are* fictions-- fictions backed up by a gun.

But the state and its laws are so much more than a fiction backed up by guns. These fictions are also backed up by expectations, desires, social sanctions, *even hopes and dreams*. The result? *Voluntary compliance with rules, and their enforcement by the ruled on the not-so-voluntarily compliant*. Though the state and its laws are fictions, we ignore them at our own peril, *and they have predictable operationality*--unlike a band of criminals.

The legal system uses logic as a tool for self-policing so that the system is persuasive, self enforcing, attractive, and thus reproductive of hierarchy. The rules are *not* arbitrary, capricious, and/or universally or even generally abusive--class bias (race is a proxy for class in the U.S.) is implemented systematically and operationally, with plenty of places for opt-in and opt-out - and thus a remarkable flexibility. Otherwise no one would obey *or ensure others obey*. Finally, not only does the legal system use logic as a tool for self-justification, it uses the rights formed out of that logic as the means to the end of the good life. The system is not only *persuasive*, it is also *attractive, self-enforcing, self-reproducing, and sustainable*--it produces and reproduces hierarchy and structures conflict.

Criminality isn't sustainable because it disincentivizes production and raises transaction costs. Criminal conflicts are completely unstructured. People have rights because they *need* them (or at least think they do), and because they are, at least sometimes--maybe even often-- a useful way to organize the social body, to channel social conflict and make it less and less destructive. And so it goes.

*

Remember: A good story starts with a killing or a kiss. It then explains its causes and consequences.

The cause of the kiss?
Greed.

The consequences?
Death.

HERE ENDETH THE LESSON

About The Author

Eric Engle has studied law in the US, France, and Germany. He has taught law in France, Germany, Estonia, Russia, Ukraine, and Bosnia. A Fulbright law specialist and polyglot Dr. Engle really likes words.

Remember to learn more at
amazon.com/author/quizmaster

OTHER BOOKS BY ERIC ENGLE

amazon.com/author/quizmaster

CAN I ASK A FAVOR?

If you enjoyed this book, found it useful or otherwise then I'd really appreciate it if you would post a short review on Amazon. I do read all the reviews personally so I can write what You want! You can also write me an email with questions, comments, or suggestions: eric.engle@yahoo.com

I really appreciate your feedback!
If you'd like to leave a review then please visit the link below: amazon.com/author/quizmaster

Thank you for your support!

www.ingramcontent.com/pod-product-compliance
Lightning Source LLC
Chambersburg PA
CBHW070908220526
45466CB00005B/2178